Beauty for Ashes

- Words for Autumn -

Poetry for All Seasons
Ana Lisa de Jong

ACADEMIC PUBLISHERS

Hardcover: 978-1-98-855778-6
Softcover: 978-1-98-855779-3
Ebook: 978-1-98-855780-9

Published in New Zealand

A catalogue record for this book is available from the National Library of New Zealand.

Kei te pa-tengi raraunga o Te Puna Ma-tauranga o Aotearoa te whakararangi o tenei pukapuka.

Table of Contents

Forever is a Room

Forever is another room.
It is behind the garden's hedge,
too thick, too high to surmount.

It is behind the memory,
the way it teases us in dreams
to see further than the eye.

But, more than a storehouse for our histories
or a wellspring of our tomorrows,
it is a road

with no end or beginning
that we each find ourselves travelling upon,
even here, even now.

The boundlessness of our soul
a clue

that this life, this garden hedge,
bed, cup, hands we each hold
will all fall away

as we carry on as pilgrims on a journey.

Our forever room, large
as a prairie, wide with its roof of sky
and distant hills, paths into the blue.

Our forever room, small
as a drop of dew teetering on the edge,
in which we are enclosed,

the knowledge beyond too great for fathoming.

And yet, accompanied,
we are not beggars on the path
but pilgrims with a staff, a light, a bed

at the end of each long day –
and company in the remembering,
in reunion, the recognition in waiting faces –

and the eternal light,
the embrace in which we're held.

Introduction

S unset shows us there is nothing more beautiful than the dying of the light, particularly in those few moments when the sun dips past the horizon and we think the display is over. And then the sky, the fields, the foliage pick up the sun's last glorious flaming rays in a beautiful final encore turning fiery red, pink, gold before all settles into darkness.

I have often thought autumn the most beautiful month, in that the days are mild, the sky is a soft blue, the light has lost its harsh brightness of summer. The weather is that little bit more settled and predictable. And the display knocks your socks off. A little like the sunset at the very end of her show, before darkness covers the land.

We think, when we survey a brilliant sunset, or a swath of deciduous trees in full colour in their bright red, orange, gold leaves, 'What have we done to deserve this – this awe-inspiring moment?' And ask ourselves, 'Why is this act of dying, this final encore before bowing out so glorious?' Perhaps we think it more appropriate that dying be done quietly, discreetly, modestly?

But maybe a lesson for us in this display is that life is just so beautiful to live, despite the hardships and the griefs, and the world so wonderful, that we should not want to leave it quietly, should not want to just bow out but to flame up and burn in the departing. To leave a residue in our wake, as a carpet of golden leaves.

Rainer Maria Rilke's poem 'Autumn' is resonant of this time of falling leaves and life's slow departing:

The leaves fall, fall as from far,
Like distant gardens withered in the heavens;
They fall with slow and lingering descent.

And in the nights the heavy Earth, too, falls
From out the stars into the Solitude.

Thus all doth fall. This hand of mine must fall
And lo! the other one:—it is the law.
But there is One who holds this falling
Infinitely softly in His hands.

Yes, there is one *"who holds this falling infinitely softly…"*. And we know from the cycle of the seasons, and the night's arriving and the morning's return, that autumn is a prelude to winter, which is but a quiet sleep before the spring, when everything returns with new life, warmth, and vigour.

Sara Teasdale wrote in her poem 'There Will Come Soft Rains,' – *'And Spring herself, when she woke at dawn, would scarcely know that we were gone.'*

Life does return, and that is the hope of the turning seasons, and why I think autumn can bow out with such beauty and grace, because she knows in the very blink of an eye, the leaves will turn to mulch, to soil, to then become a rich bed for spring growth. Life's green continuum will carry on. And the glorious sun knows as she sinks beyond the horizon that as a planet we will travel round to bid her welcome again.

So if nature knows that there is nothing to fear in death and loss, might we take comfort from her amazing display in these autumn seasons of our lives and allow the season to speak to us her secrets as a wide elder might pass wisdom to a tribe before passing through the veil.

This book of poetry, *Beauty for Ashes – Words for Autumn*, is one of four books in a seasonal series whose titles are drawn from Isaiah 61, the prophecy of Isaiah concerning the Messiah.

> *'To all who mourn in Israel, he will give a crown of beauty for ashes, a joyous blessing instead of mourning, festive praise instead of despair. In their righteousness, they will be like great oaks that the Lord has planted for his own glory.'*

Isaiah 61:3

Yes, if we are great oaks, we know that we can let our crowns become radiant with turning leaves with the knowledge that their shedding will provide the nourishment for next year's new leaves.

Nothing stays the same, but everything still continues, a prevailing truth that can allow us to appreciate autumn for who she is – brief lived and beautiful.

Ana Lisa de Jong
Living Tree Poetry
January 2021

September 1 – Northern Hemisphere
March 1 – Southern Hemisphere

Colours

Every day, season has its colours.
None devoid.
Every season its light.
Lengthening days or longer nights,
light still comes. Often the more
cherished for its shortened appearance.

And colours new or faded
have their own presence.
Enough to draw tears, arouse our memories,
bring disquiet.
What do we do about the changes in hue?
We can only witness. It all happens without us,
although we take parts on the stage.

Constancy

Sometimes we need the quiet,
constant things.

Like water that flows,
ripples over pebbles,
in eddies and currents of a stream.

Sometimes it's the certain things,
the sure and solid things,
like rock.

Or it's the translucent things,
the clear fluidity of water
running over stone.

Sometimes we need the message,

unspoken but clear,
in the way water turns
and circles and twists,

is so busy running
but somehow exudes calm
and strength.

Perhaps it's the rhythm,
the constancy of movement,
the way it mimics dance

that causes our hearts to slow
in response.

Perhaps it's the clarity that,
despite the surface turmoil,
we can see right through to underneath,

where all is still
and undergirded.

Seeds

Are you just a little angry, ruffled feathers,
or tail high like the cat, fur on edge?

I woke this morning out of sorts
that if licked, I might taste of salt.
It's hard sometimes not to nurture a seed.
To give it space on the shelf, to ponder it.

Which could be wise for a time,
but then there is Khalil Gibran's
advice to plant,
which already gives a strange relief.

That early, before anyone is up,
I might heed the birds to the great outdoors.
Settle my hands in the comfort of dirt,
dig a hole, cover it.

And tomorrow I think I'll wander the garden
trying to recall where my seeds have been sown.
I do hope though I won't till next season,
that they're given time to become something else.

"In the autumn I gathered all my sorrows and buried them in my garden. And when April returned and spring came to wed the earth, there grew in my garden beautiful flowers unlike all other flowers. And my neighbours came to behold them, and they all said to me, 'When autumn comes again, at seeding time, will you not give us of the seeds of these flowers that we may have them in our gardens?'"

Khalil Gibran

Autumn

Autumn's here,

like a woman shaking out her skirts
of dust.

The breeze is as fresh as
air caught up in dancing gusts.

And the sun, a little lower now,
hangs bright and resolute.

Not ready yet to take her leave,
turning the leaves on their edge

a little bit more gold
under her demure glance.

And the clarity of everything
seems like some last ode

to summer's long haze
of days.

Like crystal that's been taken out
and shone.

No one minds the winter's coming
steady grip,

when summer retreats into the wings
with such a long last encore.

It seems when seasons change
we're somehow ready for their turning.

Anything that lasts too long
gets tired.

The spring,
that in another hemisphere is appearing,

is causing our summer to give out,
like dancers weary of their fling.

But all is good,

for the earth is readying herself
for the digestion of autumn's shedding glory.

And we, we yet anticipate
the dreaming in our sleep.

The imagination that winter's blanket
will draw in and cover,

for spring to unfold
as some yet amazing feat.

Grace's Secret

Grace has a secret for you.
She has everything packaged,
stored.

As in her private garden
she leads us, dancing muse,
to where she holds us captive
by the way she's corralled the sky,
drawn the sea.

Grace has an assurance,
she has everything catered,
invested.

In her loose raiment,
hair lit by the sun,
she is the treasure
we hadn't dared to pray for,
the hope we couldn't believe.

And though we cannot see the end,
the wind,
she is the feeling of the breeze,
the promise of a harvest stored,
planted, nurtured.

Our redeeming seeds,
our future drawdowns
secured,
no matter the state of the earth
or our soul's need,

Grace has her secrets.

Short Sighted

I am short of sight.
Are we not all
somewhat compromised in our vision?
Our circle small
to the extent our sight can stretch.

I know the more I fear
the tighter yet the circle I draw,
that it's a wrench even
to let the ones I love
out from reach.

But it's on the periphery,
out beyond love's cocoon,
the place of safety that I would make
that life is lived
and lessons laid out for the learning.

So I, short of sight
must find my trust
in what I cannot see,
out beyond the bridge of knowing,
where God works now with rolled up sleeves.

And while I stand
wringing my hands,
unused to emptiness
and turning in the space
the width of my arms –

I must draw the will
to put down the lens,
where at best glimpses are seen,
and draw the curtains in
to settle here,

surrendered,
upon my knees.

Plenty

Lack can be a good thing.

Enough in itself
when we focus on the plentiful,

the gifts still amongst us.

Do we not remember

how the fullness of bread
forms itself from yeast

and warmth

and the soft, kneading hands
of love's attentiveness?

Might we
in our lack

measure what we have,

count the things remaining
here at our disposal.

The stuff at hand
to give yet,

in ways we hadn't imagined
or considered in our plenty.

Yes, our palms might sweep across
an emptying shelf,

find an egg, flour, rice,
basics to make nourishment,

and then our hands
might find feet

to lace in shoes
in which to walk

with sole intent
to our neighbour's door.

Yes, did we ever think
the gifts we are given

were to keep.

Perhaps this is the rainy day
for which we have been hoarding our treasures.

What indeed happens to the
things we don't forfeit.

I know there is much I've thrown out
from too much excess,

and a spare shelf
might instead

clear a path for miracles.

Seen

I want to tell you that you're seen,
sitting there in the dark.
The blue's a veil, the clouds will shift
in a giving way to the moon.

The light, though now just a forgotten thing,
will all of a sudden appear.
The clouds playing skittles with the wind will push through,
and the moon arrive like the sun.

But in the meantime you're still seen.
Loneliness is a shadow cast by grief's lengthy visit,
and tears a shield
to soften the remembering.

These things will shift like clouds at midnight
chasing and unveiling the moon.
Yes, joy is a thing too fickle for some,
a frail presence too soon.

But God will come on little cat feet
as mist receding at noon.

On Trial

To act with justice but to love mercy,
walk humbly.

How to walk sometimes
with the scales balanced?

The cups held steady.

Justice something to be prised from our grip,
so intent are we on the administering.

Whereas mercy,

mercy is not poured from one cup
without the emptying of the other.

And what is love but the antithesis
of withholding?

The hospitable one pouring,
absolving –

serving us tea.

Judgement

By judging I seek to keep you.
The shape I know, the you I want or think you should grow into.

By judging I seek to keep you
in that place you were, the safe place with set parameters.

But I remember now how all learning is done outside the comfort zone.

Judging, far from keeping you,
will build a wall I'll close myself behind.

Will make me blind.

September 11 – Northern Hemisphere
March 11 – Southern Hemisphere

Gentle

Come in gently.
Feel the lie of the land before you step.

We don't know the burdens others bear,
everyone wearing their smiles for fortitude.
So come in gently.

Is it not better to fill a space with your parting grace
than to have to sweep up breakage from a misstep?

We do not know, we can never fully understand,
so we cannot presume the topography –

coming as we do with our positions,
and without a map to follow.

Cracking

I am cracking open
so I can be sea glass,
gathered,
turned into mosaics.

I am being cut,
laid out to dry as petals,
colours retrieved
before they're spent.

I am being run down
as mown grass,
to become a stretch of emerald green
where birds arrive for worms.

I am a vase on a windowsill,
its beauty in the way it captures
the light of foliage and bud,
the way it holds itself out

as an offering.

Growth

Ah, if there were no night,
could God indwell the beauty of the morning
in a way that we could perceive the light?

And if there were no night,
could change occur
in a way that brings the seed to stir,

and break,
to emerge from the earth
as something else?

Ah, if there were no pain,
could anything be done to further our
growth

or would we simply be it,
finished?

We are not finished
and the journey
not complete.

For morning to come
we must turn a full circle,
rising again at dawn's light.

All Sufficient

A Prayer

Prayer is our armour,
peace a shield.
Your presence is a guard
against the night.

Great Mother,
we drink from your breast.
Great Father,
we fall into your deep well
of all sufficient love.

Like the woman who asked for the water
that would forever satisfy,
so she would not have to venture out,
we ask for water over our heads,
baptising,
pouring from our limbs,
our skin.

Silence is an eye in a storm,
silence is the deep powerful centre,
the engine room of energy,
of quiet power.

In your silent presence is our peace
and grace,
our prayer-forged shield.
And from your endless sustenance we drink
to the depth of our need
and fill our water jars to overflowing.

Faith By Sight

We cannot force faith.
Like happiness, faith is fostered
in moments that look very much like a giving way
of expectation.

We lift our eyes
to the ever-changing weather,
the inclement climate,
the clouds taking turns with the sun.

Somehow, even though the heavens change
and stars fall out of the sky
to burst at the edge of the world,

we trust our world to hold.

Faith is something we can sometimes drop,
like eyeglasses.
We search around a little bit blind

until we find them,
grasp our fingers round,
return them to our face.

The Great Silence

In the great silence
the flowers seeded and grew,
the rain fell, the land took a breath,
exhaled.
The sun turned on its wheel
heedless to the forecast doom.

In the great silence
the leaves folded, took their queue
and detached from the branch
to become the first fruit
of a fallen carpet
destined for mulch.

In the great silence, north and south,
the seasons changed,
exchanged batons.
The earth on its axis followed a path
long trodden,
defined by millennia past.

And in the great silence
the people burrowed in,
appeared on occasion for air
and breathed secure for knowing the earth

carried on its resolve,
resolute in purpose.

And in the great silence
the planet rested,
the people rethought their focus
and slowed,
unfolded from the weight of lament and fear
and returned as a world newly formed.

And in the great silence
the people rebuilt their altars,
with the memory of the lost
freshly engraved.
And with the lessons of the earth
and their treasures preserved,
the people conceived of a new way.

Circling

Can we circle in?

When we are spiralling out
so much so that we lose our balance,

how do we draw in again
to the still firm central place.

Sometimes there are questions yet
for which we think the answer's found circling out

in the vastness of space,
a wide blue canvas.

While each star shining looks
alike to another,

and we can we feel as small as specks
floating upon a foreign landscape.

Can we then circle in,

slowing, slowing,
smaller, smaller,

that we might feel the universe decrease
to match the pace of our attentive steps.

Might we take nature's queue
and return again to the central circle,

the growing place, the quiet seed,
within which lives the universe's blueprint?

Everything we ever accomplished,
everything we ever imagined

formed in that sacred hidden place
to which, when we return, we are received,

known, and all questions shed,
the answers here all along.

Hospitable

There is nowhere to hide.
To live hospitable to ourselves and others
is to receive ourselves whole,
to give ourselves broken.

To be fallible, to be alive.
To live hospitable to each other
is to open our cupboards and drawers.
To see inside, to lay it out empty.

To say 'this is what I have and what I don't.
These are the hopes for which I strive.
This place of struggle is still a place of wings,
of overcoming.'

The thing about love
is it always rises from ashes.
To live hospitable is to allow the burning.
Be swallowed whole, come out the other side.

Longing

Some longings cannot be satisfied.
Some thirsts cannot be slaked.

Some hungers gnaw at our inner selves,
that it's easier to deny their rumblings.

Some longings move us without compulsion.
Some impulses drive us without consent.

While knowing we're profoundly blessed
we quiver for what we have not got.

Some questions ask more than they answer.
Some feelings arise from their own accord.

Some years are seasons that arrive without endings,
and some endings are not easily sought.

Some longings impel us to action.
Some cause us to curl and lie still.

To quiet ourselves until our needs subside
knowing they can't be filled.

Some longings serve simply
to remind us of our humanness,

as bodies not yet made perfect
or haunted by missing limbs.

Some longings just serve
to bring us to awareness

of the completeness of one
who holds our questions and our answers.

The one who gives us imagination
and hearts forever restless

and knows the world
in which our longings form and move.

Who knows that sometimes all we can do
from drowning in the waves

is hold on
to the one who leads us

by the long way home.

Loving

But I love,
and I know you never said
I couldn't,

that you made this heart
a beating organ.

But I love,
and didn't know that
in the loving was the learning

of what love means
and what it doesn't.

I love,
and I know you never said
I couldn't,

that you made this heart
a vessel pouring.

But I love,
and didn't know that
in the loving was a grief

for what love can keep
and what it can't.

I love,
and I know that you never meant
for me not to be

a heart beating,
a vessel pouring.

But I love,
and didn't know that
love would teach me

to the degrees it crushed,
asked I bled.

That to be a an organ beating,
a heart pouring
itself out,

I had to know what it meant
to give and not be fed.

That to love
was more like the fountain springing
from the deep mountain source.

It didn't need the one it watered
to be anything other

than loved.

Gentle

God needed a way to explain that gentle isn't weak,
that gentle is fierce when pursued,
when made the standard.

God wanted to show
that everyone comes to themselves when led soft,
like a horse wooed, readied for the saddle.

God wanted to show that gentleness is a head turned
and a grace given,
whilst not always being a pardon.

But with expectation delivered
in encouragement's tone,
the revelation of something different.

Yes, God needed a way to walk
in the world,
shoes tailored for peace's proclamation.

And God needed a means to explain that
gentleness is strength restrained
and that weakness is power let loose.

And so God, in infinite wisdom
made woman
to teach, nurture, bear forth –

beauty in the turn of her cheek.

Fluid

Everything is fluid
when we think of it.
We are more water than substance.
And it pours from us,
in tears, blood, sweat.
In our passions,
in the heat of love,
in the waste released.
Ever liquid in, out.
Mingling together
as rivers meeting.
In the giving of our lives over
to one another.
Each day's pleasure and pain
asks for our immersion,
in our tending of the young,
the infirm.
We cannot escape the truth
that in life's basic needs we sink
or swim.
That while we might dry our hands,
our affluence has a way of shielding us
from this –

this reduction again to water,
that we are ever drawing
and releasing.
Ever giving ourselves up to
as it carries us along.

Stretching
– A Poem for Chronic Pain Sufferers

You know how the tree reaches out?

Ah, she plants her feet,
stretches up her arms,
takes her weight.

And in her trunk is all her strength,
centered.
She feels her roots, endorsing them

to channel deep,
to make the earth her grounding place,
her firm foundation.

And where there is need
for shade, or fruit,
fresh foliage,

she feels the stretch,
an earnest wish to be more than this,
for her reach to meet her best attempts.

And when she feels the pull,
her trunk responds at the core
to everything she's tried

and failed,
all the ways she's gained and lost,
everything for which she longs –

the joys and griefs tied into knots,
all the things that given grace
she would find the strength for.

But,
you know how the tree reaches out?

Ah, she plants her feet,
stretches up her arms,
takes her weight.

That when the seasons turn
and the pain of trying
becomes a grip too tight to loosen,
then release becomes
a slow discerning,
a necessary lesson –

an answer for all the things
run their course,
the battles lost.

That the worst of griefs,
the loss of leaves,
is a carpet rich to feed her roots.

And in the fall,
her trunk absorbs the very life
needed for her sustaining.

Yes, you know how the tree reaches out?

Ah, she plants her feet,
stretches up her arms,
takes her weight.

And in her trunk is all her strength,
centered.
She feels her roots, endorsing them

to channel deep,
to make the earth
her grounding place,

her only true foundation.

Blue

You know you can lose things
in the blue.

Things that have outstayed their welcome,
like worry and angst.

You can hang yourself upside down,
watch your pockets empty –

or take a jump right up
and scatter things about like leaves.

And some things on losing
are not worth the finding and retrieving.

Some things, like winter lows,
need a blue sky arriving to send them sideways.

And when the sun shines
like the golden haired heroine she is,

well there is much that we keep
meant for burning.

Another Choice

What if justice fell over,
would grace take her place?

How many causes do we back,
how many bones pick bare?

The grudges that we hold
and turn to every angle,

if held against the light,
what residue would we see

but dry bones turned to dust?

What if justice fell over?
Would there be less offence taken,

given,
less choosing of sides.

Have we lost our voice
if we can't raise it above a whisper,

be heard above the din,
the crowd and its followers?

What if everything that wasn't grace
was laid down?

Perhaps everything is just a further chance
for emptying.

And every place we find ourselves,
another choice to love.

September 26– Northern Hemisphere
March 26 – Southern Hemisphere

How?
– Lines to my late father

I went and asked you how you did it –
let go?

I think you said something like,
it wasn't something that you did

so much as surrendered to.

Not that choice was yours.

And in the surrendering
you discovered how

choice can be something
over-rated.

That the big picture has always been

the one we never see.

So I go and ask myself, how do I do it –
let go?

And, as though you haven't gone,
I hear you say,

'you just fall in,
close your eyes,

open wide,
embrace what is at hand.'

Marking The Path

I carry ribbons
in my pack of days.
And when I reach a tree to define my path,
I tie it round, mark a lesson,
towering high.

I wish it were so easy.

Not the ways trodden with regrets,
wisdom learnt in retrospect,
footprints already settled deep
in earth –

and the journey,
turning, turning.

That the colours glimpsed between tree leaves
are ribbons hanging
limp on trees
that have not moved.

But in my pack are red, pink,
each shade of blue,
and sunshine yellow.

That to feel the bark,
like a friend old,
is to tie the colour of the heart split open
to the measure of its love and need.

Perhaps I will not be fully there
until all is red
and the journey understood as progress
not defined by distance

but by how we circle the labyrinth
deeper in.

Although I had thought to see new scenes
with lessons learned behind,
this old ghost with its green leaves,

fresh growth of bark on trunk,
I mark with red threaded with
the wounds of life –

the sign of a heart laid open.

Patching

I'm just glad I got through another day
with a little bit of beauty.
It's like patching a quilt.
You choose the swatches of fabric you wish to keep.
You select the thread.
You carry on with immortalising it.
The memories you hope to retain
made predominant,
the colours made from feeling.

At night you pull it up to under
your chin or over your cheeks.
Who can be cold or without comfort
with the best kept?
Turned into the things we've
chosen to recall.
The rest discarded to the pile
of cloth for which there might
be a place one day,
a reason why.

In the meantime,
a 'comforter' needs the things to
which our heart leans.
The softness of a safe embrace.

The enfolding swell of down,
the cool of cotton.
The colours of the feelings that feel best.
Yes, to get through another day
is just enough
with beauty in it to retain –

enough of which
to make a keepsake.
The rest against which
we can close our eyes.
Discard to the floor
anything which doesn't fit
or disturbs the vision.
Thank God we have a mind to choose,
a heart to discern
what it is our lives are made from.

The Kingdom

The Kingdom of God is like a bird
whose nest is blown down in a storm
but sings still –
the resource at its disposal
all the world God owns.

The Kingdom of God is like a hand
opening and closing at God's pleasure
and will –
trading the jewels of wealth and privilege
for the pearl of greater worth.

The Kingdom of God is deep
as a cavern in rock
the eye cannot see –
moving when we do, ocean currents drawn
and propelled by forces beneath.

The Kingdom of God is a whistle,
a call to sheep
who know its register –
who come and go according to a voice distinct
to any but their owner.

The Kingdom of God is a seed,
a piece of broken bread,
wine poured forth –
a tree, its branches fed in living sap,
and a dry earth drinking.

The Kingdom of God is a person alone,
divested of props or security,
restored with nothing
but an empty hand – a walking staff,
a map to eternity.

Drawing Light

The people wouldn't let it.
The rising dark shadowed the hills
as the threat of storm,
air heavy as lead.

The people wouldn't let it.
The people shut the blinds,
drew the shutters closed,
lit each candle, settled in.

When the wind turned itself up
in an effort to frighten,
the people drew the light
tight around, turned on music.

And the people
picked up pens, instruments,
paints and brushes,
cameras, journals, paper for letters,

every medium of hope
their hands collected.

The people took all the dark notes
and mixed them with light

to glowing colours,
remembering how

when the night draws in,
the outside has no effect
on the heart
and its capacity to self-determine –

to create something different
with the cards fallen,
to draw beauty out of
patterns.

Yes, the people knew
without a shadow of nuance
that in the whirling wind lay calm
at the core, energy to harness.

And the edge of darkness
creeping at the curtains
could do little else but highlight
the light.

Though it seemed to trespass,
the people wouldn't let it,

drawing circles with light.

Old With Me

Grow old with me,
the best is yet be.
The best to come.

We thought the best
arrived when first
we met,

young things
on the cusp,
the brink of falling in.

We thought it better
yet
when two became entwined,

joining at the roots
to branch out and
make a house.

Under which
seeds were shed,
and seedlings grew.

We thought the best
was here,
in the shade, the sun.

But grow old with me,
the best is yet to be.
The best of these years behind

have made a bed,
that when we start to lose
our leaves, our strength,

we will see
how the smiling
does not stop,

memories enriching
everything arriving yet,
everything stored up.

For My Body

For my body
I would step
around in a thousand circles,

like the sun sets
or the moon orbits
the earth.

Who is in love
with whom?

For my body
I would follow
the way the light hits

the upper side of leaves,
the trunk,
the grass spread.

Who is desiring
whom?

For my body
I would sing
low,

trill high,
the way the birds
sing their morning chorus.

Who is calling out to
whom?

For my body
I would,
but perhaps the flesh

is as the rose's blooming
flush,
petals shed.

We're to give up the frame
for the substance burning –
reducing

to the eternal essence.

Anointing

Tears,

running sap
from the tree's trunk,

poured milk
from the heart's overflow.

Sweat, for the reach of our arms
beyond their stretch.

A wet stream followed
to the soul's interior,

eyes cleansed
to perceive its depths.

The wound's seeping
to aid in its healing,

rain falling to soak
a parched, shrivelled earth.

Did we know in our griefs
how the healing of the nations

would depend on tears
and our willingness

to pour ourselves out,
stripped

and bleeding.

October 4- Northern Hemisphere
April 3 - Southern Hemisphere

Messages

I am combing the air for scraps of things
I'm not ready to put down.

Is restless the right word for want not quite relieved?

Or needs unspoken
for there being no language adequate,

eloquent enough
to enable the expression?

I know I have one foot here,
the other searching,

like toes underwater
feeling for shells.

I have one mind here,
one heart.

But there is another part of me
embodied,

with wings.

By the stream, the hill,
under the stars.

What she's always wanted
I do not know.

Crossing Over

How do we cross into the year,
with peace our compass and courage our hiking stick?

I've heard suggested
that we set our minds on heaven –
and yes, the mountaineer has a goal
though shrouded yet in mist.

But where in looking forward
do we find the present?
Where might we spread ourselves
as a space wholly encompassed?

My friend speaks of the eternal things
that some of us confuse with heaven.
When life is hard
we have the salve of imagination,

that we might see through the glass
a brighter day called faith,
somewhat like a hunter
searches for game.

But my friend speaks
of an eternal present.

Like a heaven placed gently
in the hand.

I think it is only with this
I can attempt any movement.
The year, too big a thing
on its own.

October 6- Northern Hemisphere
April 5 - Southern Hemisphere

Seasons

How often are the things we carry
made of ashes held in the hands?

Whole in memory,
carried with careful intention.

How often do we look
through yesteryear's lens –

make the mistake of perceiving something
as solid and real,

as continuing?

How often can we face ourselves
as lone sojourners,

walking on the ashes of everything
surrendered?

There is no containing anything.

Even the things we are given
are only ever lent.

And any sense of possession
is all on our side.

How often are the things we carry
too heavy?

Perhaps we were not meant to cleave
to anything.

Yes, the idea of everything as illusion
is not truth.

But everything has a season,
its long day in the sun.

Presence

Your presence abides.
Like the rock
off which the water runs.

Your presence sits
as the birds flock near,
undisturbed.

Your presence lies surrendered
and therein finds its strength
in undoing.

We ask questions
flung into the night,
dark –

asking
which star to draw down
has the answer written?

But you sit
abiding,
a rock in the river running.

Your presence beckoning,
saying – 'here,

leave your health,
leave your fears,
your poverty and need,

the sorrows
that threaten to overspill –
watch them fall, run away

with the river's tumultuous flow –
watch only what is left here
standing –

the presence under all.'

Scales

You break the scales.
You strain at the seams of our understanding.
That the heavens you have made can house you
is too much to fathom.

When we know our place as less than nothing,
dust on the scales, or vapours rising,
gone by noon.
We wonder then the reason for anything.

We look at the moon,
the whirling solar systems,
the measurements we've learned,
and earth too small for a pin's head.

We wonder then
how small a thing must be
before your attention's diverted.
And yet you came,

in obscurity, in such vulnerability
and utter nothingness,
that power became a thing small and hidden,
to cross barriers.

And even in death, you would find a means still
to be with us,
that the heart might hold in the smallest seed
the one who established the heavens.

Yes, you have broken all the scales
and torn to shreds the seams,
that there are no laws or means
to explain you.

And yet, we all soften,
no words needed,
as one beholding a child at the breast,
the symbiotic mystery of mother and son.

The Christ child who laid down his crown
to cross light years
and yet travel less than a hands-breadth distant
from a father who's not drawn his eyes from us.

God's Garden

I bemoaned the lack of things.
A certain symmetry, or correct aligning.

A certain youthful vignette
from memory.

A certain flush, a just bloomed,
rounded skin of apple –

a store-bought peach,
blemish free.

I bemoaned the silver thread.
White-water crest of waves

through a river
long and dark,

its only shine now
caught under starlight.

But God said,

'time –
it's immaterial.'

Hair that greys,
skin that sets in its downward pattern.

Eyes that look out
from tissue paper wings.

Whose definition
in the end matters –

determines the rightness of our beings,
the thing that defines us as ourselves?

We might bemoan the ending of things,
the turning of the seasons.

The certain ease
in which we faced the day.

But now, in the slowing down,
the reflective passage of autumn,

we see how the seed
became the tree, and the leaves then falling.

And we might bemoan our frames,
our many irritations –

but in the tree's skeleton
under the grey leaden sky,

its limbs contrasting
against the light,

is the shape still of the seed,
the beauty of a youth outgrown.

So much so that I cannot bemoan
the ending of anything.

For whose determining
sets beauty's worth?

And usefulness is always God's decision.
Energy gives way to wisdom.

And even here yet in the mulch,
God is working, planting.

Failing

You will fail.
But if you fail doing what you love,
then what failure is that?
You have chosen the better thing,
the way of living.
Which in essence is succumbing
to Life.
Loss, gain, who's counting?
As soon as you count
you're measuring the blessings.
At what point then does loss
turn to gain, and when do gains run out?
Throw out the yardstick,
the balancing scales.
Understand how it's all gift.

Falling

When we have learned to fall like the leaves,

when we have learned to move like grass
to the flow of wind,

when we have learned to mount
the precipice,

as a deer on a ridge –

or as a dancer might pirouette
on the head of a pin –

when we have learned
to blossom

at the touch of sun,
moisten in a passing gust,
dissolve in the mist.

When we have learned
all these things,

we might have the courage to walk
on two feet,

out-of-doors,
bridging all the 'what if's' –

one foot here
and the other already

in eternity.

Dying

You are dying every day
a little more.

Each day you plant your feet
from bed,
solid on the bedroom floor,

you have died a little in your sleep,
and your solidity
belies the fact a part of you has left.

Each day is a journey on,
making pieces
of your patch-worked quilt –

your own design,
no pattern fixed
or pre-defined.

Yes, each day
you are drawing something
together with a silver thread,

something to travel on with you,
made from everything of meaning
here.

And in your dying every day,
you are opening up more to life,
to continuance.

And everyone to whom you
leave your dying light
will use it to light new wicks.

And when you are ready,
heaven will have fully opened up,
like something you recognise –

something you have been making
with needle and thread,
laid out there for you in wait.

And in the receiving you will see
how life has indeed been
prepared for you ahead,

from the deposits of everything
you have surrendered
and all the love you've spared.

Degrees

We say goodbye in degrees.
And that is the sad, sweet thing,
how each step is a degree away.
A turn.
Like the earth from the sun.

The sun means nothing less
than it ever did.
But in surrender to life's
momentum the earth must give way
one day's long length at a time.

Had the earth ever said to the sun
I can't leave,
the sun would make it
that the choice isn't hers.
So instead we hold our dignity.

I know I will swallow everything
that can no longer be done
in the day's long turning.
Where it goes I do not know.
We say goodbye in degrees.

A Forest

Whatever you might believe, life is forever.
You were made a leaf on a living tree
in a forest to eternity.

Though a day's length might be determined by the rounding of the sun,
a season by the passage from growth to decline,

and the elements beyond your influence.

The fact that you are more than a first flush,
or even a last golden hand, is something
the body understands, the soul intuits.

Does the singing bird that builds its nest
and nurture its young trust also in the branch,
the sturdy tree?

So you might know yourself as more than a
leaf that takes its cue to part the stage
upon a falling curtain.

We are all more than the substance of which we're comprised
at a singular point in time.

We are that, too,
to which we're attached,
to which we return as living matter,

the mulch that breaks down to soil to feed the roots,
this forest in which the singing birds are ever
lifting their dawn chorus.

Ever migrating to, from,
in a great circling formation.
In this pattern of life, death, renewal.

Love Follows

There is a thing about love.
You don't need to be with people to feel it.
Love follows.

And love has already arrived
where we each are going.
It's the host preparing our place before us.

And love is a thing far reaching
that you can never decide your way out,
or go somewhere it is not waiting.

For love is always preceding and expecting us
and bringing up the rear.

The Path In The Middle

Verily the middle way is the path of love.
The way of peace, of patience, of deep accord.

Where, as we walk,
the healing comes gently,

swifter as we relent, relinquish our wants.
As we give way to another's wishes, hopes.

Accommodate misfortunes, faults
and yet still believe for another's sake.

This healing which finds us in the middle
will radiate from its heart,

that each become caught in a beam of grace,
making a way for love.

Established

That could be us.

There is always a place on earth
with a still pool,

a river reflecting the sun,
a place to dwell in safety,

a mountain vale,
a wildflower sanctuary,

a meadow for rest,
a place hemmed in

by natural boundary lines.

That could be us.

When the fire is raging,
when the world has gone to blood

and flames,
and tears that rival all the joy

we've felt,
lost in the space

of a moment left
undefended,

a season we can't control.

Then that myth
that we had a say

comes back to us
to stare us in the face,

while outside
everything burns,

and it's hard to believe
then

in that still place
that carries on

despite us.

But it could be

that there is always a place on earth
with a still pool,

a river reflecting the sun,
a place to lie looking through leaves,

a mountain slope,
a refuge for birdsong,

a stream to refresh,
a place secure,

established.

October 18- Northern Hemisphere
April 17 - Southern Hemisphere

The Road
– For the Traveller

How often do we set the path,
a goal in mind,
to discover something else?
Yes, who knows what's down the road?

And how often is the way,
far from set in stone,
a future undiscerned, folding out,
like the road does when we turn the bend.

And how often do we stop to pause,
get our breath,
see a scene we did not expect,
like stepping stones, or possibilities.

Yes, when we are given a GPS,
map of the world,
we find there are a thousand stops
between our origin and destiny.

Each a many flowered gift in itself.

Beauty Chaser

I will chase beauty until I find her,
though she has fallen from the sky.
I will find her in the cracks between the pavements,
the bright bloom escaping the hedge,
the white-tipped waves on the horizon.

She is almost the more beautiful
for surviving against the odds,
and she does not cost the earth.
She is our antidote to everything that takes from us,
by the fact that she is free, akin to grace.

And if no condition is placed on what defines her,
she can be found
in every corner of a room, yard,
on the sill, in a jam jar,
in a break between clouds.

We can even wear her.
She has a way of transposing herself upon the skin,
that we will feel undressed without her
and will search again and again
until we can gather her round.

October 20- Northern Hemisphere
April 19 - Southern Hemisphere

Going Out

I'm going out
and I won't be home until I'm happier.

Less hungry for want of
what I do not know.

I hope to find it by the river
or on some bend somewhere on my walk.

I don't know,
but I will be looking

for the unexpected thing
looking back.

Knowing that
the treasures we collect

are seldom brought home
in sandy pockets.

A note caught in the wind,
or leaf or flower bud unfolding,

is best left where discovered.

But I, myself,
I can come back

a little higher and wider
for what I've found.

A little heart warmed,
or soul stirred

that my want
may settle down.

October 21- Northern Hemisphere
April 20 - Southern Hemisphere

Pink

I didn't know I was pink,
or blue with a soft coral edge.

I didn't know the world and I
could change colour
according to the sky.

Perhaps it's the trees
with their red tips lit.

But tonight the world exhaled
as lovers collapsing
into quilts.

And softened as a babe
replete at the breast.

That I thought,
if this is grace
I now understand.

My hands flushed
as by candlelight,

imbued with
the colour
in which they're enveloped.

This setting sun entreating
the world to yield,

as grace upon skin,
pores wide
open.

Alchemist

Do you see
how mountains erupt out of oceans.

Do you see how tears can make a flood,
but from the depths we still emerge.

Do you see how seasons fill their purpose,
though we might prefer the sun benign.

Do you see how everything is clearer
and cleaner for the rain.

Do you see how nothing in nature
is without design or reason.

That everything has its cause
and effect.

And though circumstances appear random,
God works in us,

amazing alchemist,
for our benefit.

October 23- Northern Hemisphere
April 22 – Southern Hemisphere

Taking Turns

We slip in and out of view.
One curtain opens, another closes,
a newborn cries, a child weeps.

The sun sets, sinks
and then emerges again
as though nothing has occurred.

That life has a way of turning over
is both brutal
and hope filled.

We need something
to look death in the face
and obstinately resist it.

We need something,
even when the odds
are set against us,

to persist like the greening of spring,
the thawing of snow.
The world looking entirely new.

But still, we'll take our flowers to the gravesides
and light candles for remembrance.
For prayer vigils.

No returning spring can remove a present pain.
Though the morning arriving
is the dark night's certain lifeline.

And the child weeping
will yet smile.

And the woman with her infant
will tell the truth again
of how it's ever been

a baby who's restored to us the world.

Goodbye Is Not

Goodbye is not always
what it seems.
Not always a cause for sorrow.

Nor a loss to be assumed
and worn upon our frame
as a cloak of grief.

Goodbye is not
what we would often make it.

Gratitude is good.
Like a carpet that unfolds to more,
it paves our way.

But our focus on what we've lived
will keep us
slowed in that place

from which God
has already moved.

Goodbye is not always
forever.
Not always a giving up.

Nor a holding to us tight
the blessings
we've been given.

Goodbye is opening the hands
in anticipation.

A stretching of the legs
before a long walk,
a restocking of all that's been good.

To fill our pack
and sustain us
for the journeying.

Goodbye is an opening
to a larger world.

A graduation.
That this place that nurtured us,
that has both given and taken from us,

has made us ready
for the next thing.
Like a child who lifts himself from his knees

to stand and walk.

And goodbye is not always
a walking away.
We take with us all we've been given.

The world expanded
now takes in
all that's new and old.

With tears, we smile and survey it all.

October 25- Northern Hemisphere
April 24 – Southern Hemisphere

Sunday Visit

I coveted a visit
from a friend today,
so pulled up a chair.

And set out a pot of tea
to steep
and then pour.

I looked for the sun,
to seat us where the warmth
would meet our feet.

I then called myself to come
as a friend might
bid welcome at the door.

And then I sat
and took a breath
and shared a smile.

Like an embrace
from someone
I'd been sorely parted from.

And words unravelled
as thoughts
kept long unexpressed.

And my friend
lifted her tea cup,
still and attentive.

As circles forming their
spirals in my mind
poured forth,

like crumbs
now left forgotten
on our plates.

And the sun lengthened
its rays upon the floor,
while music in the background broke into my thoughts,

until eventually a child called
that I must rise and take my leave
collecting my cup

and rinsing in the sink.

Fireflies

Sometimes I catch them,
these words in the ether
as fireflies in the dark.

I catch them in a net,
briefly loaning their light
to transcribe something unheard.

Sometimes I catch them,
these words off your tongue,
lit gems in the rush of speech.

And I take them and store them
when no one is looking,
in the fertile ground of my heart.

Sometimes I see them,
these words in your eyes,
and I dress them to keep them close.

And still sometimes I set chase
to court and lose them.
But it's enough to know they exist.

Yes, sometimes I catch them
and more often do not –
but it does not matter at all.

These words dancing on the edge
of vision and thought
to a music heard from far off.

A Passage

Is not the passage to eternity,
as a canopy of trees
under which we shelter,
and walk, and rest,
and live?

Is it not a length of road
that stretches,
that we cannot see beyond the hill
but know what must be there
by what we've seen?

Is it not an arcing encompassment,
like one branch curving
toward another,
but letting in light
and air to breathe?

Is it not love
that does not wait until we arrive
but comes to meet us and walk
with us
upon the road?

And is not
the passage to eternity right here,
in leaves that turn
to drop as burnished gold
at our feet?

Blanketed

The sky is but a blanket to cover us
in this garden of the world in which we play.

I can hear your laughter ringing out
like youthful memories of summer evenings
at the edge of dusk,
when the first stars emerged
and voices would be carried for miles.

Yes, the sky is but a blanket
in this garden in which we live and love.

I can see you stretched on the grass,
the lazy humming of a bee or swatting of a fly,
the only distraction from the pleasant sense
of sun burnishing skin.
I could reach out to touch your hand.

Yes, the sky is but a blanket
in this world in which we play.

All of us running at the bottom of the garden,
hiding behind the wisteria, paddling in the stream,
everything is drawn out here forever,

until a window opens
and someone's called home for tea.

Yes, will you meet me here,
in the garden?

I will not have forgotten your face.
Everyone here
is one of us here,
and though the shadows fall,
we know each other's names.

Do You See Me?

Do you see me coming

around the corner
with noiseless feet?

The wind announces my presence
or shields it,

that the pines might carry on singing
as they've always done.

And that I can be here
on the trail,

where no one has stood for so long
nor stands now.

Today I told a friend
how to close our eyes is to take ourselves anywhere.

And that thought has taken me
upon a path a million miles from me,

with feet that make so little sound
that nothing moved for my being there.

Nature,
whose heart beats without pause,

might have stopped to receive me
as one already welcomed –

but who could say?

Certainly it's been enough
to sit

and watch the sunset falling
like burning leaves set alight.

And to hear the sound of the night owl echoing
across the valley.

Did you see me coming?
The sound may be me

or it might just be the pines
forever singing.

Now that I recall the ease of flight
I can close my eyes

and open them everywhere else.

Reworked

What if we were wrong
and the aim is not to grow,
or at least
not to perfect ourselves,
as pots hardened in a kiln?

What if we were to expand
instead
and then crack slowly open?
What if we were made to break,
and start again?

What if to shatter,
just now and again,
felt like some kind of enormous relief?
What if we were to melt
down as snow?

What if perfection
were established as the myth it is,
and the crushed became the
oil to
anoint the earth?

What if we could hold
the broken pieces of us with
reverence,
regarding the intrinsic worth
of each?

And then offer them up
surrendered,
cast back into clay
and reworked to
another shape?

What if suffering were the
path to salvation –
this road not always chosen
but which, in reflection,
might become a better way?

What if opportunity
and new beginnings are things
wrung out of the old,
like precious jewels retrieved and
melted down as gold?

Yes, what if we were wrong
and the aim is not to be
right,
so right that no one questions
our holiness?

What if sometimes to
be wrong is right
and to be weak is strong

and true growth sometimes
is to fall with the leaves?

And turn like the seasons
into mulch,
and earth,
and the soil
to sustain new life.

The Holy Broken

Forget the mask.
Forget the forehead set.
Forget the stiff upper lip.

Let yourself tremble,
shake like the windblown leaf,
speak your truth.

Though it might be to admit
failure,
fear or pain.

Life has its vicissitudes,
and we can sometimes start to roll
like a stone gathering speed,

or may feel
the pounding of waves
as driftwood afloat on the sea.

But forget the mask
and the face set like flint,
the lips that do not move.

Cast off shame.
For the tears that fall
are made to cleanse.

The crutch leant on
to stand
is to aid rehabilitation.

And the heart that breaks open
reflects the naked eye's
silent plea,

that there be no incongruence
between action
and speech.

Yes, forget the mask.
And the poker set face,
the mouth sewn tightly shut.

Come out of hiding,
for the world to see
your naked face.

The world needs us each,
the strong and the often weak,
the holy broken people –

In community.

Joy Is Bent

I'm good at pretending
and so are we all.

But joy is bent
and love oftentimes a strident noise

of notes played off-key in
inexpert hands.

Yes, joy is bent,
not perfect.

Or it could not be
in the relief

of a softened gaze
after a sharp retort,

or in the small crises that teach us
how love is forged through tears and smiles.

The touch that says,
'we start again',

that those we bruise and hurt
we kiss and heal.

For joy is bent,
so that it returns again,

and love is learned
that even those that feel the deepest

must learn to develop
the means of expression.

And even then,
love will sometimes hit a strident note,

as a flute at the lips of one
still learning its art.

Yes, we're good at pretending
that all's well and together

when in truth all is broken
and re-mended.

And love both the calm before a storm
and the sun that shines after rain.

Joy is bent,
that it returns again.

So Beautiful

The skin is just a covering for the bones,
so the flesh would have an encasement.

So that we can stand and move, and
have the body do our will.

But why, why so beautiful?

The skin is just a fabric of soft silk
stretched over hills and hollows.

It is just a ream of cloth, bolt of cotton
that has been put to purpose.

But why, why so beautiful?

In the folds,
the hang of drapery,

the moulding to curves,
the falling down inclines.

The skin is just a covering for the bones,
the blood and organs.

That we can function as living beings
with lungs and breath,

hearts and sense.

So that we can put our bodies to use.

But why the endings at our nerves,
the way our senses stand on edge?

And the way we move,
feel against each other's surfaces,

why, why
so beautiful?

Swaying

Did you want to be swayed
by the wind,
by the external things?

Do you want to know how everything
that is solid runs underneath,
and through?

Do you want your thoughts
to lift you up or down,
to live rudderless?

Do you want to give credence
to impressions that come and go,
like mist before the breaking light?

Do you want to believe,
believe in how what can be bent
can never be broken?

Do you want to know how,
despite appearance,
all that matters is solid and substantial?

The human spirit,
a triple woven rope, flexible,
made of enduring stuff,

like the heart that can be bruised
and then renewed
as new skin growing.

The tree that broke
its branch at the wind's behest
is still ripe with sap and strength.

So let go of the thoughts
that would determine doom,
the worries based on lack and fear.

Not everything we think is true
is real,
and not everything we fear is imminent.

And the things that in the mist
appear to take on
fantastic shapes,

we're to let them remain
the insubstantial things they really are,
and to drift away

with the coming light.

Connected

We are connected.
The spider's web
that bridges a gap
and reaches into space
from one branch to another,
its silken length
the means it travels
teaches us

that storms,
whether from nature's storehouse
or human made,
cannot bear up against
one hand that reaches out to another,
or hearts across an ocean's span,
which bow and lift
in prayer.

As the spider lays
its wondrous web
to show us
that not all we think we see is real,
sometimes the light reveals
a net wider and stronger

than what we first might have believed
and placed our faith in.

And this net
that bridges the gaps
between what we see
and what we don't,
what we live and what awaits,
what we hope for and what we fear –
this bridge, stronger than it looks,
holds.

And if it does not,
the spider that has curled
and waited out the storm
steps out again in faith
when light returns,
making links into space
to rebuild
its intricate world.

Things

Things save us.

Yet, we're told to hang on to faith,
to not put our trust in the concrete,

the things susceptible
to change.

We are told to hold our beliefs safe
in heaven,

in a tomorrow
eventually won.

Not an earth that fails us,
inconsistent

at every turn.

But I wonder if things

are not sometimes
just what we need.

That sometimes
we need the solid,

the here and now,
substantial.

The strength of a towering trunk
and its overarching branches.

The sun,
which each returning day

deems us worth its brilliance.

And these walls,

which keep us warm and dry
and shut out fast the night.
And the doors
that we can lock,

and choose to open
or not yet.

Sometimes we need the blankets
we can pull high over our heads.

And the strong arms or chest
we can lean into,

encircling us in the dark.

Yes, I know

we are told to trust
in God in heaven,

not place our hope
so much here,

among the broken things
of earth.

The here today
and gone tomorrow.

But I'm aware how I've found God,
and a reason for continuing

a thousand times over again.

This hope,
resting upon the imperfect

and a world forever opening its arms.

Will You?

Will you take my heart back
to where the land meets the sky,
to where the kiss of heaven
touches earth's upturned brow?

Will you take me in my imagination
to places we haven't been,
where life is not a forgetting
but a remembering?

A recalling through the mist
of the true shapes of things.

Will you help me forget,
and take me to see
wonders illuminated in my vision,
things hitherto unseen?

Will you come on the clouds
and on every rising sun,
and each glowing shade
brushed against

the great canvas
of your turning world?

Will you take my heart back
to where you and I together
haven't been,
but in the blink of an eye can always visit?

Will you come and renew to me
the awareness of
mountains which rise to your hand,
and seas that move

like lovers
remembering each other's geography?

Will you come take my breath away
and then restore it as something
I always had inside,
singing along with the earth's?

And will you travel with me in my imagination?
There's no distance
that can't be bridged by
clouds that hide boundaries

and then recede to reveal the world
as something boundless in our midst.

To Fall

To fall is human
and to err
a part of life.

How the sun rises
to then be obscured
by cloud,

that it might almost appear
to be offset
from course.

Yes, we do not know when
we might walking,
all of a sudden trip.

Like the sun
leaving too soon.
But it's always a surprise.

And we are so much better
at lifting another up
off the floor.

With the easy grace
of the tall
and the strong.

But when it's us looking up,
bare-faced,
with hearts unveiled.

We might think our
countenance is now
as dark as a vanished sun.

But we might be mistaken.
Guilt can sometimes be
too quick to erase errors.

But if we can keep ourselves
open and unshielded,
as when in free fall,

we might find
that to err is human
and to fall divine,

when the truth
bores in
like light from heaven.

And we see ourselves
naked,
and in great need.

Then learning can begin,
and relationship previously untested
be newly forged.

Yes,
to fall is human
and to err a part of life.

How the sun rises
to then be obscured
by cloud,

that it might almost appear
to be off set
from course

to the unlearned eye.

You Love Me When

You love me even when
I'm all angles
and brittle bones.

And I realise how

it takes energy
to nurse a hurt
or uphold a frown.

So, you love me,

and soften me
as kneaded dough
under your gentleness.

That I flex
and stretch again,
within the moulding of your hand.

My tightness shed
as you tend to me
as lover and friend.

Finding the tense, bruised spots
and ministering
your healing balm.

And I realise how

I cannot not soften
and smile,
and spread

as warm bread
rising
under the warmth of your tenderness.

The Work of Grief

It's the work of grief
to walk two paths.
To live the present tense
and travel the route
our hearts would take
if choice were ours.

It's the holy work of grief
to acknowledge the cost
of loss.
To weigh up what's left,
treasures in the hand
now spent.

It's the sacred task of grief
to bear witness
to grace
that comes on silent feet
to spring-clean rooms
of residual dust.

And
it's the sacred role of grief
to reroute us on a road
now taken shape

upon the remains
of former gifts.

Grief's task is not done,
and often
the fallowed earth,
newly turned,
brings with tears
an Eden remembered.

But grief,
the shadow side of life's jewels,
shows us how to regroup,
and outlive loss
by turning
to the light.

Crack

The wind is high
and we can hear
the hollows through the branches,
like reed flutes
echoing in long laments.

The cold has come
with an Arctic breath
to cause the bones
to fuse
and set in one place,

that if we were to stretch,
we might fracture
and break.
If we were to weep,
we might freeze as water is trapped.

While across the world
it is summer yet,
the land warm
and beating as a heart,
flesh flushed and rosy as from sleep.

The birds that sing
and the sun with a benevolent gaze
belie the way
the earth feels the shock
of tiny ricocheting shots.

And spasms akin to
an ice shelf moving,
and melting beyond
the realm
of human sound.

Until we hear a sudden crack,
not unlike a gun let off
in a quiet place.
Not unlike an earth
rupturing at the core.

Home

What is home?

Is it a solid thing
felt underfoot
or something we carry on our back
or in pockets, as well-honed stones?

Is it the face of one long loved
or a landscape made familiar
through sight and touch?
Is it dust

or earth,
sifted through fingers
staining the skin with the colour
of remembrance?

Is it stone,
wood, fire, air –
or the elements of love,
the warm embrace of blood and kin?

Is it song, to bring quiet solace,
or lament
to recall the heart's
constant ache?

Is it a memory, or a road
upon which we walk,
continually away,
each step a move more distant?

Is home for some,

a gulp in the throat,
the frozen tear unshed,
the thing we pick up and put down again
in a foreign land?

Is it everywhere,
in the wind, or just here
in this home-shaped hole in the heart,
this lost heritage

of the dispossessed?

November 12 – Northern Hemisphere
May 12 – Southern Hemisphere

Peace Candle

Lord make us instruments,
candles burning for peace.
Make us steady lights.

Power not in strength
but in the unwavering glow
of a soft, gentle flame.

Seeing how
one candle in a room
is enough to dispel the darkness,

I wonder what a million
burning flames and hearts might do
to halt the onset of the night.

To turn it bright as day.
As a dawn rising,
rather than a sun descending.

Lord make us instruments,
candles burning for peace.
Make us a steady light

whose power is not in might
but in the influence of a
million lanterns linked.

Healing rays to
herald the breaking of heaven's dawn
upon us.

Who bear its light
with an unwavering
gentle flame.

A Line

I don't believe anyone does not believe.
Life takes faith,
in our rising of a morning,
our continuing.

Life takes resolve,
courage of a sort that
draws from hope in life's giving hand,
dares to trust beyond loss.

Those who confess to non-belief
perhaps have not measured
the faith needed
to reach a point in time.

How each time they rose
from failure or grief
was another vote,
a stab at life.

Like the fisherman casting a line.

And the God who said
our faith would be rewarded –

I think knows
how for some faith has been
a momentous climb
from the ground to their feet.

And they might not call it that.
But to toss the line at all
there must be hope for something
at its end.

I call that belief,
though it might be unspoken.

Cursive

It is like cursive words upon the page,
this way we live beside,
linked but separate,
in running ink.

It's like the tide
that turns back upon itself,
the curve of a wave ocean bound
becoming a long ribbon of river.

Or it's like flax,
how in the hands of the weaver
it becomes a mat, or a kete,
a carrier.

Something greater
for its plaited strength.

And it's like rope, three stranded,
or a knitted vest,
a comforter for the knees,
or the young.

And it's a blanket
made from many threads,
under which our limbs, our arms
are words linking in cursive.

The Answer

Did you want me to give you an answer?
I am sorry I didn't hear the question.
And I didn't arrive with answers.

Life speaks to me in little truths
that don't bear witness to anything else
but the thing that they stand on
in that moment.

But all these things find their source
in love
or I wouldn't believe, or speak,
or write of them.

But I don't ask for understanding
so much as faith, that the thing I know
I know is enough in itself
in the moment it is apparent.

And like some faithful witness,
I will try to draw it like I see it,
for isn't art in truth
different to each discerning eye.

So it does not matter so much
how you read it,

though the blessing is both of ours
when we meet at some mutual 'Yes'.

Then for a moment the little truth that's shared
surprises in how it facilitates connectedness,
like some sudden mirror
revealing a larger whole.

But as soon as you ask me for a position,
I will tell you I never heard the question.
And that the answer, if it's anything,
is only ever one.

One word in the many millions,
one word resounding.
And if you ask me what it is,
I might just say to listen.
That the answer is clear,
as though there were ever a question.

A Problem

Sit with a problem.

Anything that arouses
anger, fear, distress.

Sit with it
and watch.

See how it does not stay the same,
though the problem might persist.

See how the way it's held
has a bearing on its weight.

And the shape of it evolves
as we turn it in our hands.

See how a day or night
or week might help

to hold it
with greater ease.

And another's eyes and ears –
see how it is perceived.

And then sit still
and watch again.

Perhaps with time and company
it might continue to evolve.

Until when surveyed afresh
we might find it part dissolved.

Yes, sit with a problem
and ask, 'what gift is this?'

Anything that arouses anger,
fear, distress,

sit still
and watch.

See how we may
in some way have changed,

though the problem might persist.

Patience

We must be patient with our days.
The ground's prepared and then by all appearance
lies fallow as an empty field
under water and rain
before the farmer has a crop for harvesting.

And the woman making bread,
weighing all her elements,
kneads with patience,
allowing the yeast to ferment,
kneading again, that the dough will rise.

There are steps for sowing, reaping, gathering.
Measurements for the science of baking,
for the makings of flour, water, salt, yeast
to merge and change,
become something else.

And, if the farmer works
to keep the birds from his seed
and the baker selects a warm place for his dough,
so won't the angels for us clear the way forward,
sweeping the road.

We must then wait patient within our days,
which sometimes appear to stretch
as a field out into oblivion,
under a sky bleak and
rains returning in their season.

But there is nothing wholly quiet about
the minutes stretching, collecting,
the hours multiplying as grain in a field,
when there are elements in the mix for our
establishment,

readying themselves for appearance.

Half

When I walk

I am half me at that,
less even.
My eyes look straight ahead,
no hindsight.

The past mostly a blank,
apart from imagination.

But when I walk,
I feel a memory through my ankles,

not of shape so much
as sense,

like rising mist
from which I step,

not entirely myself –
more the composition of many,

and it's simply my turn
to be here.

Perhaps it's something like
a bloom on the clematis growing wild.

And when I fade, the one who takes my place
drinks from the same vine,

of which we know the taste,
its liquid sap in both our veins.

When I walk

I'm aware I'm half there,
at that.

And it does not matter,
not one drop,

from whence I came
or where I'm gone.

The vine,
even when it eventually depletes,

has dropped its seeds
in the bush, deep and green.

Te Puna O Te Ao Marama
– The Wellspring of the World of Light

The hills cast green shadows.
Where the sun hits
rounds and hollows are defined
in full clarity.
Like the face of love
is familiar, cherished
in kin we recognise.

Yet the hills cast long shadows,
green crevices,
carved valleys of shade,
hidden mysteries
without language,
shape or form
to fill our vision.

We look into the dark
and are swallowed by immensity,
the questions hanging bare,
unanswered.
Instead we learn contentment
with the gist of all we know.

And the things without language
or form
are like the mist that hovers,
or the soft rain that settles upon shoulders,
as the feathers of a cloak
we do not know we carry,
nor what beckons.

But from the shadows
something remote resembles us
and looks out
to where we stand
backlit by the light,
and we are known then
by all we do not know.

And the hills stand as pillars reaching up
where we in their midst
are encompassed in their house.
Though the language and the memories
are not voiced aloud,
we hesitant guests at the door
stand welcome.

A Change of Heart
– A Poem for the Planet –

'God will take care of us'.
I know, I've said it,
meant it,
cannot not trust, somehow.

God makes a way.
Paths through the sea,
and manna heaven sent.
John in the desert, preaching,

preparing us
for one who, with his hand,
would scoop up mud
and open eyes.

We have a habit, I think,
of walking blind.
Cheerfully
stating our faith.

I wonder why then
John had to shout,

exhorting us to turn,
repent.

Are we so inclined to inaction?
Is sin so personal,
or in collusion,
is the wound deeper?

Perhaps the day has come
where a little dirt might be
the thing in the hand
to change the heart.

I wonder...

For Beauty

I think beauty has become the new bread.
There was a day we scanned our emails
for bills, for discount sales, for those things
we'd forgotten we had meant to do. And now:

Now we check each platform we belong to
for snippets enough to feed on.
To gather together to make a meal to sate
the gnawing of our stomachs, our hungry mouths.

And beauty has become a need,
like water, or shelter.
The beauty of friendship, of connection
in a world a little fractured, frayed at the edge,

that beauty becomes like thread for
mending tears,
or a doctor's ministrations
to set our broken bones,
to give us faith in healing.

Now beauty is as much a comfort
as a hope.
A hope of something exceedingly better,

158

or even just the ordinary becoming
commonplace again.

For who would use their time on beauty
unless there were a chance
for our continuing?
Who would waste good bread
to serve beauty on a platter as sweet cake?

Diversions

Ah, you can give me a word
like water, or birth,

anything a prompt for opening.

And I will want to expand,
to express everything seen,

but with there being so many
impressions,

I must choose where
to narrow in.

When to choose
is to briefly greet

and then send away
the untapped sensations,

the openings to feelings,
unknowns,

wondering all the while
to where, to whom

might the poetry have led
had another route

been chosen.

In The Right Paths

At my beginning.
At my end, which is not an end,
only ever a beginning.

At my front.
At my rear.
Fortified, and held secure.

At my feet.
Leading my steps.
Placing them, one after the next.

Guiding me in righteous paths
for your own sake,
that I won't misstep.

For I know your glory
is greater than my own
ends which I might prefer to seek.

And you would lift me
on your shoulders,
so that my walk

is in your steps.

Glimpses

You ask I follow, but I can't see you.
Gone in a flash between leaves, like a sudden gust.

And I don't know what is it I'm asked to follow.
My own life, in footsteps,

this disturbance in the undergrowth,
here and gone as the foraging birds.

And what is the nature of this thing
that hints its path for me?
This fleeting glimpse
soon shrouded by leaves.

The part of me perhaps
that imagines a myriad of possibilities.

This part of you that attends to me.

Perhaps it's simply that movement itself is life,
and any measure forward is an opening into newness.

And any hint need be enough to trust the places we find ourselves in,
in this forest of the world in which we live.

Giving Thanks

Today I can hear your 'thank you'
as a great resounding chorus on the breeze.
To bring me to my own knees
aware of everything I'm blessed by.

And I wonder if you can hear my response,
or the earth even.
I think I can hear the earth's small intake
of breath, of release – of relief.

There being so much loss and death.
So much returning to dust, that the
earth needs our thanks for the
task of its receiving.

It hurts with us, and we,
with our gratitude,
take up our fork turning compost,
these ashes of our days,

that they might break down
to something good.
Something too, that future generations
might call themselves blessed.

For what is thank you for,
the light, the dark?
These elements to build the soil upon
which our children walk.

Thank you, thank you, thank you,
all of it grace.

Arohanui

Arohanui.
If love is liquid,
then we are all made of her.

And this shower, been and gone,
means we each swim in liquid air,
making its way back to heaven.

And the molecules in me
do a little dance to sense the ones in you.
A kind of coming back to home
in this one river with all its many tributaries.

This air, in which we flow and move,
reaching for one another,
not dependent on a solid footing
but able to weightless float.

And these clouds on their trajectory
east, south,
with us adrift on their coat-tails.

Yes, if love is liquid, we both move in her
and are made of her.

She, the aroha which gives us wings,
and the wet earth to keep us grounded.
And still humming underfoot
along her network of veins.

Arohanui, her sound, that of a call
which has an answer echoing,
though we might think of it as only
the wind, the rain.

And her touch,
as lovers underwater,
all arms and legs, and mouths wet with joy –
and all this body in between.

Reasons

It's in the way we see.
The way we stop to note,
the blessing is not so much
in the planned,

the up ahead intent,
but almost instead
in the little scenes at centre left,
the sacraments upon the way.

The heaven meeting earth
flashes,
like shooting stars
too frequent to recognise,

but when seen with open eyes
and stilled soft breath
are known then as
the most real things,

the many reasons we're here.

Ribbons

You leave such a trail as you set.
Your golden orb sending all the clouds to flame.
And the blue of sky
against the soft rose pink
belies that you've already made your retreat.
Left the room with ribbons trailing.

Yes, you become most beautiful
as you take your leave,
as a woman might turn
the round of her cheek
to the too frank gaze of a man, smitten
by her lowered lids.

You have such a way of beckoning us forward,
that perhaps you're simply given
to show us how,
when it's our time,
we won't necessarily desire to tarry –
but even now

could follow you over the hills.

Burning

I am a burning tree
catching the flame,
sparks flying.

For every leaf surrendered
to the fire,

for every shrivelled
ashen piece of me,

a new shoot,
fed by my old remains,
emerges.

Burning tree,
alight with holy flame,

teach me,

that death and life is a
constant cycle turning.

And as we are consumed,
we brightly light the hill

upon which in another day
we grow.

In The Midst

It is hard to believe in the midst of it
that the mist is a veil.
Or in the dark,
that the dark is a blanket.

Whenever we cannot see our way
it is hard to imagine beauty exists
somewhere still
not far from us.

Even when tracing back,
seeing our path cross hills and vales,
a dip in the topography
can seem a descent to darkness.

Although up above
all might be light.
Exquisite even, for the mist, the sun,
in her arriving and departing, her continuing.

Sometimes the sun will come find us,
scattering the mist to fragments.
Other times, she will gently lift the blanket,
waking us into hopefulness.

171

Whether we reach her by foot
or she arrives, dazzling or tentative,
we realise the dark is just a covering,
the mist a harbinger of morning.

Extended

The grass is wet underfoot,
the showers passed.

The sun slants through the trees,
falls in sheets
upon the field.

The soul is something like

a blade of grass,
extended straight,
looking up.

It moves to the wind,
lies down underfoot,
is, on occasion, cut,

then grows again,
vigorous.

Oh, to live like grass,
surrendered,

evergreen in light and dark.

Lightning Source UK Ltd.
Milton Keynes UK
UKHW050953090223
416655UK00001B/12